A JUNIOR SCIENTIST'S GUIDE TO

GENETICS

WRITTEN, ILLUSTRATED AND GRAPHICALLY DESIGNED BY

SONYA KULKARNI

To my family,
for your unconditional love and support,
for sparking my love for science,
I couldn't have done it without your
genetic material.

To patients and physicians,
for your contributions and discoveries.

And to you, thank you for choosing this
book, I hope you enjoy it!

PREFACE

Dear reader,

Growing up in a household with two parents in the medical field, I have been availed of many privileges, such as having unrestricted access to literary texts of my choice: everything from children's books about science to the medical holy text that is Gray's Anatomy. However, my interest in genetics was sparked when I discovered that I was diagnosed with mild-to-moderate bilateral hearing loss at birth. My condition is hereditary, which, as you will learn in this book, means that it "runs in my family." I was inspired to learn more about genetics, as a result, and discovered the sheer magnitude and implications of this exciting field.

We are now living in very interesting times where humankind is reaping the benefits of decades of research. Today, instead of one-size-fits all approaches to medicine, we can create individualized treatments for patients using genetics. The future is truly upon us, and tomorrow's geneticists wield the balance of power that drives our civilization. Therefore, there is no better time to create a generation of medically literate individuals to power ourselves forward. I hope this book serves as an introduction to your foray into the bountiful universe of science and brings you as much joy as it did me.

Sonya Kulkarni

TABLE OF CONTENTS

Genetics as a career

The future of genetics

Experiments

Extras

ALL ABOUT GENETICS

Of mice and men

What if I told you that you're 85% related to a mouse? Even though humans and mice don't look alike, both species are genetically very similar. *Genetics* is the scientific study of what makes us unique and it can help us to predict, understand, and treat illnesses. While they might not have known it at the time, humans have studied genetics since prehistoric ages and are showing no signs of stopping!

Ancient genetics

A Babylonian *tablet* created more than 6,000 years ago shows *pedigrees* of horses and indicates their possible inherited characteristics.

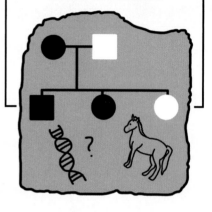

Why is genetics important?

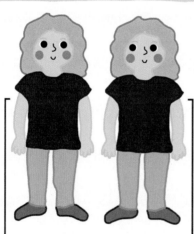

Natural clones

Some people have the same genes. These individuals are called identical twins and can sometimes be hard to tell apart!

Genetics also explains *heredity*, or how certain characteristic features pass from one generation to the next. Children are not usually exactly the same as their parents. For example, their hair color or blood type may be different. Genetics helps us understand how children can have some of their parents' features or traits, but not others. Learning genetic factors is important in diagnosing and treating genetic disorders, promoting health and preventing disease.

What if a gene doesn't work?

Genetics in animals

All animals (not just humans) can have genetic disorders. For example, here is an illustration of a mouse with albinism.

Sometimes a gene doesn't work as it should, or it works in a harmful way. This could result in a disease or a defect in a body part. You can't catch genetic disorders like the common cold, you're born with them. An example of this is a condition called albinism. It occurs when the gene that controls the body's production of coloring substances doesn't work properly.

Organisms with this disorder are often born without color in their eyes, hair or skin.

Who are geneticists?

Geneticists are medical professionals who work in the field of genetics who study living organisms, from humans and animals to food crops and bacteria. Research is a major part of a geneticist's job. Geneticists can work with a wide range of other jobs such as doctors, business people and even police officers. After earning a degree and appropriate training, anyone can be a geneticist. Maybe even you?

INTRODUCTION TO HEREDITY

To help us learn more about heredity, we're going to enlist the help of a Holland Lop Rabbit (scientific name: Oryctolagus cuniculus) named Peter. Since Peter's parents were bred in captivity, do you think they look like him?

Traits

DNA Detectives

Because DNA is in almost all of your cells, sometimes criminals can be caught just by leaving a cell from a hair follicle behind at the scene of a crime.

Traits like eye color and fur color and even risk for certain diseases are coded for in Peter's DNA. Some traits can be influenced by the environment. For example, if Peter didn't have the nourishment he needed, that could affect his size. DNA is not just one big code buried deep down in an organism, it's in the nuclei of nearly all of Peter's cells.

While we can't know for certain what Peter's parents looked like, we know that Peter inherited his DNA from them. But what is DNA anyway and what does it do?

Central dogma

The most important task for a cell is to create proteins based on codes in DNA (see page 13 to learn why proteins are so important for our bodies to function). But how exactly do DNA's codes turn into proteins? The answer lies in the central dogma of life.

The central dogma is an explanation of how genetic information flows within a biological system. It is often stated simply as "DNA makes RNA, and RNA makes protein," although it truly means that different biological material undergoes the processes of *replication*, *transcription* and *translation* in order to form proteins.

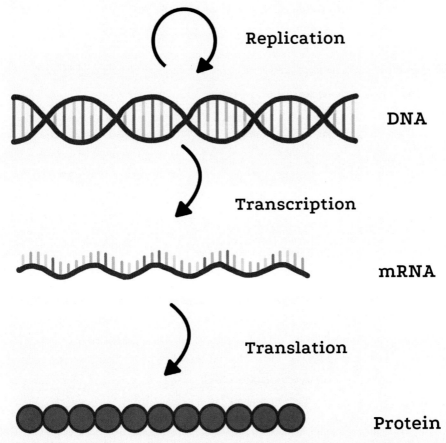

Replication

DNA

Transcription

mRNA

Translation

Protein

All of these concepts are covered in this section so don't worry if you don't understand this information just yet. Make sure to revisit this page and diagram at the end of the section!

DNA

DNA, which is short for *deoxyribonucleic acid*, is the *biomolecule* that carries all the information about the traits of a living organism. DNA tells cells what proteins to make and is made up of building blocks called nucleotides. Nucleotides have three parts:

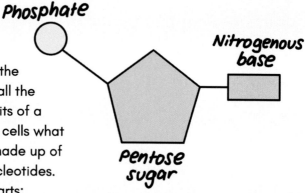

The basic parts of a nucleotide.

1. A sugar called deoxyribose
2. A phosphate (which combines with the sugar molecule to form the "sugar-phosphate backbone")
3. Nitrogenous bases (this is important because the sequence of the bases can code for traits)

The four nitrogenous bases are: Adenine, Thymine, Cytosine and Guanine. They pair together in a certain way.

Car in Garage
Cytosine + Guanine

Apples in Tree
Adenine + Thymine

Here is a helpful *mnemonic* device that can help you remember which of them pair together. Note: this is not entirely true for RNA. For more information, see pages 12 and 13.

While these four bases are present in all living organisms, the amount of bases and the sequence of those bases are different among species and individuals. That being said, it's likely to infer that the sequence of Peter's DNA bases is more similar to his parents than another species of rabbit (like the dangerous Belgian Hare).

DNA has two strands that run antiparallel (opposite from one another), meaning that there are nucleotides running up and down each side. The bases are held together by hydrogen bonds and twisted together to form a double helix shape. Portions of DNA called genes can help us understand how exactly traits can appear in an organism.

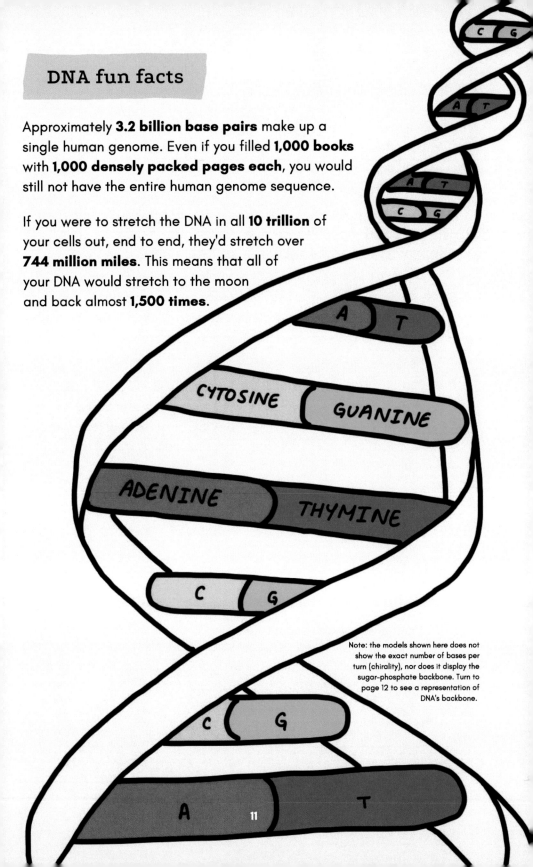

DNA fun facts

Approximately **3.2 billion base pairs** make up a single human genome. Even if you filled **1,000 books** with **1,000 densely packed pages each**, you would still not have the entire human genome sequence.

If you were to stretch the DNA in all **10 trillion** of your cells out, end to end, they'd stretch over **744 million miles**. This means that all of your DNA would stretch to the moon and back almost **1,500 times**.

CYTOSINE   GUANINE

ADENINE   THYMINE

Note: the models shown here does not show the exact number of bases per turn (chirality), nor does it display the sugar-phosphate backbone. Turn to page 12 to see a representation of DNA's backbone.

DNA vs. RNA

Usually, only DNA is discussed in introductory genetics courses. However, without RNA, genetic messages can't get out of your cells to start producing proteins. RNA is a very important biomolecule -- just as important as DNA. In fact, RNA is even hypothesized as coming into existence before DNA in the *RNA World Hypothesis*.

So what's the difference between DNA and RNA? DNA and RNA exist in all living organisms. In *eukaryotic cells*, DNA is often found in the nucleus, whereas RNA can be found inside and outside of the nucleus. Both DNA and RNA are nucleic acids, a type of biomolecule. They are made up of nucleotides (mentioned in the previous section) and both have three parts: phosphate, sugar and nitrogenous base. However, they have very different structures.

Some key differences between DNA and RNA are:
- The sugar in DNA is deoxyribose and the sugar in RNA is ribose.
- The bases of DNA are ATCG but the bases of RNA are AUCG. You'll have to modify the analogy from the previous section -- you could say Apples Under [the tree] because these bonding rules still matter. A bonds with U and C still bonds with G.

DNA vs. RNA Structure

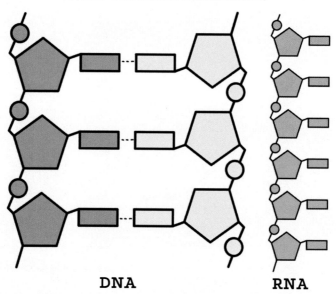

DNA   RNA

mRNA stands for messenger RNA. Its job is to carry a message based on the DNA. mRNA can leave the nucleus to take the message to a ribosome which makes proteins.

tRNA stands for transfer RNA, which transfers proton monomers called amino acids to match the correct mRNA code.

rRNA stands for ribosomal RNA, and it makes up the ribosomes that receive messages from mRNA.

Geneticists use codon charts to see which amino acid is brought for each mRNA codon. When those amino acids are joined together, they form a polypeptide chain. Proteins are made of one or more of these polypeptide chains.

Genes

Genes are essentially the blueprint for our bodies -- they are parts of DNA that can code for proteins. Proteins can have an enormous role in expressing a trait.

For example, Peter's eye color is polygenic, meaning that it's determined by multiple genes. Here, some of Peter's genes can code for proteins that are involved in producing the eye color pigment.

But proteins that are coded for by genes can play a wide variety of roles besides just determining your eye color. Proteins are involved in transport, structure, in acting as *enzymes* to make different kinds of biological materials, in protecting the body, and more!

Not all genes are used to make proteins -- these are called "non-coding genes."

Alleles

An allele is a different version of a gene and is often represented by a letter. In this case, we'll use the uppercase letter "B" to represent the *dominant* allele for brown fur. Each rabbit in the example table below has two alleles that code for their trait.

A rabbit with gray fur has two *recessive* alleles for the trait of brown fur, which is the dominant trait. A recessive allele is usually represented by a lowercase letter. A recessive allele is a gene that usually doesn't show up in the phenotype, or physical features of an organism.

On the other hand, a dominant allele is usually represented by an uppercase letter and usually shows up in the organism's phenotype. Here, a gray rabbit doesn't have a dominant allele, meaning that it can't be brown.

So in our case, if Peter and female rabbit Lucy both have brown fur then will their children all have brown fur? Not necessarily. Because there are two alleles in the brown fur trait, there are three different combinations that can tell if a rabbit has brown or gray fur.

Rabbit Allele Combination Table

BB	Bb	bb
Homozygous dominant	*Heterozygous*	Homozygous recessive
Rabbit with brown fur	Rabbit with brown fur	Rabbit with gray fur

Note: even though there's a recessive allele in the heterozygous combination, the rabbit would still have brown fur because the dominant allele "masks" the recessive allele.

Punnett squares

If Peter and Lucy are both heterozygous with brown fur, we can predict the probability of their children having brown fur or gray fur using Mendelian *monohybrid* crosses, commonly known as Punnett squares.

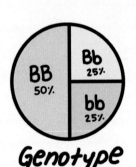

Genotype

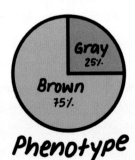

Phenotype

Punnett squares are predictions. These are probabilities, or educated guesses about what Peter and Lucy's children will look like. This doesn't mean that for every four children, three of them will have brown fur and one will have gray fur. For example, it's a probability that a child has an equal chance of being born a boy or a girl, but some families might have several children who are all born boys or girls.

Punnett's endeavors

Reginald Punnett, the inventor of his self-named genetic squares, has two species of marine worms named after him! Punnett was also known for being an avid snooker player.

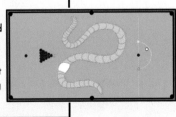

Learning these foundational concepts is essential to understanding heredity -- whether you're talking about Peter, our Holland Lop Rabbit, or what makes you, you!

Chromosomes

When DNA is compacted and wrapped around a protein, it can be organized into a biological unit called a chromosome. These often X-shaped structures are helpful when your body makes more cells in a process called mitosis and needs to transfer DNA into them.

While you can find chromosomes in bacteria, where they tend to have a circular shape, we are going to focus on eukaryotic (or more specifically human chromosomes here).

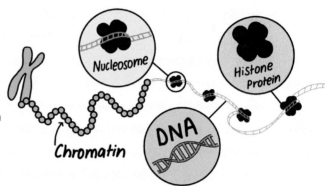

Chromosomes are made of chromatin, which consists of DNA and protein. A chromosome has intense packaging. They are formed when DNA is wound around proteins called histones -- this creates nucleosomes (which are said to look like beads on a string). The nucleosomes are condensed together until the chromosome forms a concentrated structure.

Duplication station

Human chromosomes can be represented as a single component, or can be duplicated. When chromosomes are duplicated during interphase, the newly-made chromosome is still bound in a region called the centromere. Even though the replicated chromosome looks like two chromosomes (by the way, each of these "legs" is a chromatid), we still count it as one unit because it has one centromere.

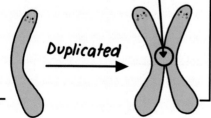

Duplicated

In human beings, most cells have 23 pairs of chromosomes, or 46 in all. The sex cells -- egg cells and sperm cells -- are considered *haploid* because they each have only one set of 23 chromosomes. This is because of how reproduction works: you get 23 chromosomes from your mom and another 23 chromosomes from your dad. These pairs form a total of 46 chromosomes. When your cells begin to divide, each of your cells gets a copy of the original chromosomes.

Chromosomes and Karyotypes

Using a piece of genetic technology called a karyotype, geneticists have the power to see all 46 chromosomes in a particular person. A karyotype is an image of all of your chromosomes where all of the chromosomes are stained (like a genetic tie-dye) and visible.

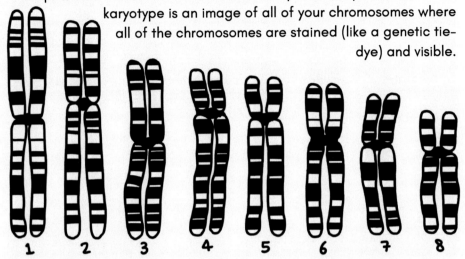

Karyotypes arrange chromosomes in *homologous* pairs (one from one parent and one from the other), which are about the same size and contain the same type of genes. Out of 46 chromosomes, 44 are called autosomes (chromosomes 1-22). This means they are not related to your biological sex and may have genes related to traits.

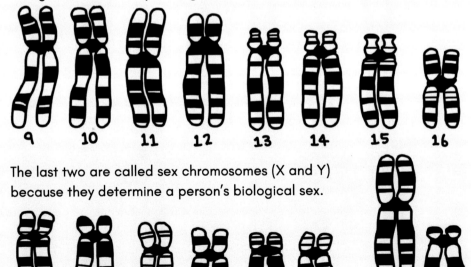

The last two are called sex chromosomes (X and Y) because they determine a person's biological sex.

A girl or a boy?

The sex chromosomes determine whether a person is biologically male or female depending on X and Y chromosomes. Sperm cells have either an X or Y chromosome but an egg cell always has an X chromosome. Therefore, when a sperm cell unites with an egg cell in reproduction, the cell usually either has one X and one Y chromosome or two X chromosomes. A cell with one X and one Y chromosomes produces a biologically male child. A cell with two X chromosomes produces a biologically female child.

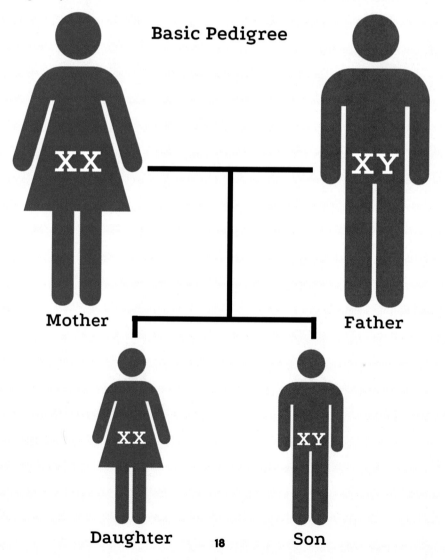

Basic Pedigree

XX

Mother

XY

Father

XX

Daughter

XY

Son

GENETIC DISORDERS

How do genetic disorders happen?

A genetic disorder happens when a gene (or several genes) has a problem with its code, which results in a health problem. Sometimes a genetic disorder occurs when a child inherits it from one or both of their parents. Other times, the disorder happens only in the child (the parents don't have it).

Different factors can cause a genetic disorder, such as:

- A change in one gene on a chromosome (called a mutation)
- A missing part of a chromosome (known as a deletion)
- Genes shifting from one chromosome to another (a translocation)
- An extra or missing chromosome
- Too few or too many sex chromosomes

Duplication   Deletion   Translocation

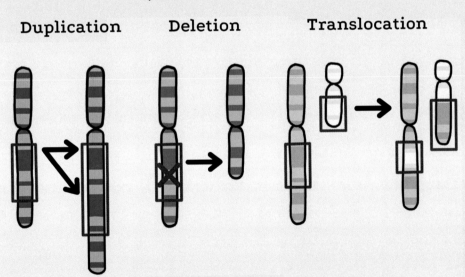

This section covers three of the most common genetic disorders in the world: Down syndrome, sickle cell anemia, and cystic fibrosis.

Down syndrome (Trisomy 21)

Most people have 23 pairs of chromosomes -- half are from your mom and half are from your dad -- which make up a total of 46. A person with Down syndrome has an extra chromosome (47 instead of 46) or one of their existing chromosomes has an extra part. This extra genetic material causes problems with their body's development.

Individuals with Down syndrome have certain physical features, such as a flatter face and upward slanting eyes. They are also usually smaller than most individuals their age. Because people are born with Down syndrome, geneticists are not certain why this chromosome complication happens to some people and not others -- anyone can have a child with Down syndrome.

About half of individuals with Down syndrome are born with heart defects, meaning that their hearts didn't form correctly. Some individuals may have intestinal and digestive problems which can be managed by surgery. Other people with Down syndrome can experience problems such as infections or even leukemia, a type of cancer. Each person with Down syndrome is different and may have any number of these problems.

Children with Down syndrome often grow and develop more slowly than their peers and sometimes need special help such as physical therapy and speech therapy. However, many kids with Down syndrome attend regular schools and may take special classes to assist their learning. Their parents usually work with teachers and individuals in society to come up with a plan for the best way to learn and grow.

Most importantly, children with Down syndrome want to be treated like any other individual -- with respect and friendship.

Cystic fibrosis

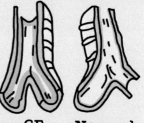

Bronchioles (lung tubes)

CF   Normal

Cystic fibrosis (often shortened to CF) is a disease that causes a person's body to make thick and sticky mucus. This can cause problems in the lungs and digestive system. CF can be mild or severe, depending on the person.

In a normal individual, the lungs make mucus which protects the airways and makes it easier to breathe. To make normal mucus, which is thin and watery, the body needs to produce a special protein. This protein is defective in cystic fibrosis, which means the body produces thick and sticky mucus instead, which can clog the lungs and cause infections.

The airways and lungs are not the only organs affected by cystic fibrosis. Mucus-producing cells line the organs in the digestive system, which includes the stomach, intestines, liver, pancreas and reproductive organs. The pancreas, for example, makes enzymes (a type of protein) that helps digest food and hormones that help absorb sugar. Thick mucus in the pancreas can make it hard for people to digest food and get all of the vitamins and nutrients they need.

CF is an inherited disease, meaning that it's passed down from parent to child. A person with CF was born with it, as it is a genetic disorder. Individuals with CF got the disease because their parents each had a gene for CF (you need two faulty CF genes -- one from each parent -- to have cystic fibrosis).

A person with CF usually works with a medical team to help them manage their disorder. This might include eating a special diet that is rich in nutritious foods to help them grow normally or by taking medications to fight respiratory infections. Along with eating right, it's important for people with CF to get regular exercise to make their lungs as strong as possible.

Thanks to improved treatments (that are now customized to the type of genetic disorder), children with CF can go to school and do regular activities. Meanwhile, researchers are working on more effective treatments and hoping for a cure in the future.

Sickle cell anemia

Sickle cell anemia is a disease of the blood. Usually, red blood cells look like round discs. However, in sickle cell anemia, they're shaped like crescent moons, or an old farm tool known as a sickle.

A round disc is the healthiest shape for red blood cells because they can easily move through the blood vessels in a person's body to move oxygen where it needs to go. But when red blood cells are shaped like sickles, they can get stuck, especially inside smaller blood vessels. This keeps blood from flowing normally, which can cause pain and damage to parts of the body.

People with sickle cell anemia may feel pain in different parts of their body when their blood vessels become clogged with sickle cells. This pain can last for a few hours or even several days and it might hurt a lot or just a little. When this happens, it's called a sickle cell/pain crisis.

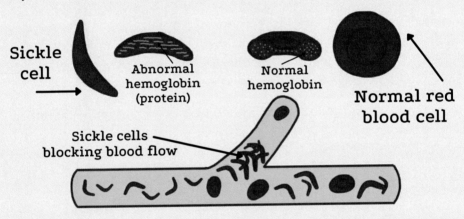

Sickle cell

Abnormal hemoglobin (protein)

Normal hemoglobin

Normal red blood cell

Sickle cells blocking blood flow

Sickle cell anemia is an inherited disease, you can't catch it from other people. Individuals with sickle cell anemia are born with the disease when both parents pass along the sickle cell gene to their children.

This disorder is treated by taking medications that help the body to make new red blood cells and prevent infections. Even though these medicines don't cure sickle cell anemia, they can help keep people who have it from getting sick. Pain medication can also help control sickle cell crises. Sometimes, individuals with sickle cell anemia need blood transfusions (a way to put healthy blood cells into a person's body).

GENETICS AS A CAREER

Professions

Committing to a study of genetics in university can open you up to a wide variety of career options at almost every degree level. Explore these options below, each of which require a different level of education.

- Forensic Scientist
- K-12 Science Teacher
- Science Writer/Editor/Illustrator
- Biotech Sales/Marketing
- Dietician/Nutritionist
- Laboratory Technician
- Laboratory Genetics Director
- Bioinformatician
- Genetic Counselor
- Public Health/Independent Researcher
- Bioethicist
- Clinical Geneticist
- Science/Health Policy Expert

Unknowns

Even though the field of genetics has come a long way since prehistoric ages, there are still a lot of problems that geneticists don't know how to solve. For example, we learned earlier that some traits are caused by several genes (these are called polygenic traits). When polygenic genes interact with the environment in different individuals, they can appear as different phenotypes and may be hard for geneticists to identify. In other words, there might be too many factors -- leading to a lot of confusion when trying to figure out what caused a disorder. However, with further research and improvements in genetic technology, geneticists continue their jobs as biological detectives.

THE FUTURE OF GENETICS

Genetics and COVID-19

In today's world, genetics is extremely important. In fact, it was genetics that allowed for the creation of the mRNA COVID-19 vaccine!

Coronaviruses, like the one that causes COVID-19 are named for the crown-looking spikes on their surface, called spike proteins. These spike proteins are ideal targets for vaccines.

As we learned earlier, messenger RNA, or mRNA, is the genetic material telling your body how to make proteins. The vaccine is made of mRNA covered with a coating that makes the delivery easy and keeps the body from harming it.

The mRNA in the vaccine teaches your cells how to make copies of the spike protein. If you're exposed to the real virus later, your body will recognize it and know how to fight it off.

mRNA vaccines might be newly available to the public but they have been studied by geneticists for decades. In fact, mRNA vaccines have been used for the flu, Zika, rabies and cytomegalovirus (CMV). As soon as scientists uncovered more information about COVID-19, they began to design the mRNA instructions for cells to create the special spike protein into an mRNA vaccine.

Future technology in mRNA vaccines could allow for one vaccine to defend the body against several diseases, which could decrease the number of shots needed for protection against common, vaccine-preventable illnesses.

Besides vaccines, mRNA has been used in cancer research to trigger the immune system to target certain cancer cells.

How mRNA COVID-19 vaccines work

Revisiting mRNA

mRNA stands for messenger RNA, which tells your body how to make proteins. Visit pages 12 and 13 for more information about RNA.

What's in the vaccine?

The vaccine is made of mRNA that is coated in a special *lipid* so that it can be delivered easily and without damage.

Understanding coronaviruses

Coronaviruses, such as the one that causes COVID-19, are named for the spikes on their surface that look like crowns, called spike proteins. These spike proteins are good targets for vaccines.

When your body responds to the vaccine, it can sometimes cause a headache, mild fever or chills. This is normal and a sign that the vaccine is effective.

The vaccine doesn't contain any virus, so it can't give you COVID-19 or change your DNA in any way.

How does the vaccine work?

The mRNA in the vaccine tells your cells how to make copies of the spike protein. This way, if you are ever exposed to the real virus, your body will be able to recognize and fight it.

Antibody

After the mRNA delivers the instructions to the cells, they break it down and get rid of it.

Genetically Modified Organisms (GMOs)

Genetically Modified Organisms, or GMOs, have had their DNA artificially modified by humans using modern genetic technology by changing the DNA of an organism. This means that we can change an organism's characteristics to our liking. Humans have been creating GMOs (of plants and animals) for thousands of years by selective breeding. Today, though, with advances in genetic engineering techniques, we can speed up this process by incorporating specific new genes from one species into a completely unrelated species.

Crops, farm animals and soil are the most common uses of genetic engineering. For example, a tomato could be genetically modified to make it pest-resistant, juicier or redder in color to be more appealing to consumers. Sometimes, bacteria are genetically engineered to produce life-saving medicines like insulin. Humans have also created wacky organisms like spider goats and glow-in-the-dark mice.

How does genetic modification happen? Here are three common ways:
1. Introducing new DNA into a genome using modified bacteria.
2. Introducing new DNA by using technology called gene targeting and homologous recombination.
3. Changing regions of a genome by using enzymes to cut out specific parts of the DNA.

Genetic engineering is different from standard plant and animal breeding because it allows genes to be moved across the boundaries of different species (for example, from a frog to a corn plant). In standard breeding, nature has invisible barriers against the transfer of genetic material between biologically different organisms. With genetic engineering, these barriers don't necessarily exist, which is why some people may consider GMOs to be unnatural.

Cloning

What if you could make a copy of yourself? Geneticists in Edinburgh, United Kingdom were able to in 1996 by cloning a sheep they named Dolly. Cloning is the process by which an identical copy of an original organism can be made. Clones have identical genes to their originals -- much like naturally occurring clones: identical twins.

To clone Dolly, the adult cell method of cloning was used. First, an unfertilized egg cell is taken from an adult female and the nucleus is removed (Sheep B in diagram). A body cell such as a skin cell is taken from a different adult (Sheep A). The nucleus is removed from this adult body cell and is inserted into an egg cell. An electric shock stimulates the egg cell to divide to form an embryo. These embryo cells contain the same genetic information as the adult body cell. When the embryo develops into a ball of cells, it is inserted into the womb of an adult female *surrogate* (Sheep C) to continue its development. So finally, after three different adults are used, the baby born will be a clone of the adult that provided the body cell (Sheep A) because it has the same DNA.

Cloning technology is extremely controversial because it raises many ethical issues. One worry is that it could be used to clone humans. Like GMOs, people may consider clones to be abnormal or raise the issue of human rights for individual embryos that could die in the process of cloning.

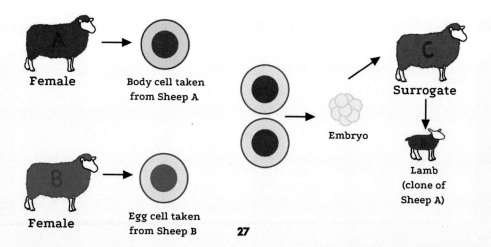

Female — Body cell taken from Sheep A

Embryo

Surrogate

Lamb (clone of Sheep A)

Female — Egg cell taken from Sheep B

CRISPR

CRISPR is the basis of a revolutionary gene editing system that could one day make it possible to do everything from resurrecting extinct species to developing cures for chronic diseases. CRISPR is built on a natural adaptation of the DNA in bacteria and single-celled organisms. CRISPR stands for Clustered Regularly Interspaced Short *Palindromic* Repeats. This means that they're just pieces of genetic code with a specific, recognizable format. These contain a sequence that shows up over and over again even though it's usually reversed (this is what makes it "palindromic"). With CRISPR, a group of enzymes can recognize certain repeats like this and break the DNA there to insert important information in the middle. These insertions are called spacers and they contain the genetic code of different viruses that have invaded in the past.

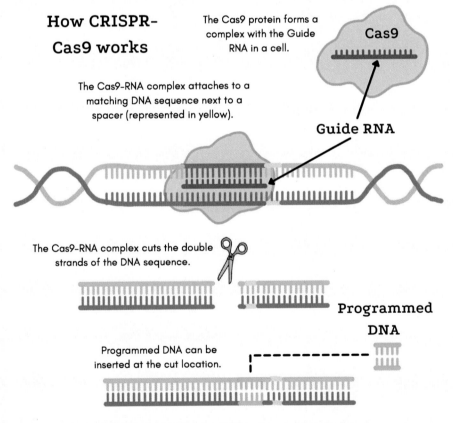

How CRISPR-Cas9 works

The Cas9 protein forms a complex with the Guide RNA in a cell.

Cas9

The Cas9-RNA complex attaches to a matching DNA sequence next to a spacer (represented in yellow).

Guide RNA

The Cas9-RNA complex cuts the double strands of the DNA sequence.

Programmed DNA

Programmed DNA can be inserted at the cut location.

Researchers first discovered CRISPR in a bacteria called E. coli in the 1980s. When E. coli survives attacks from viruses, it incorporates some of the virus DNA into its own genetic code. This is also true in a lot of other bacteria and single-celled organisms. This way, cells use these sequences as templates to transcribe complementary (matching) strands of RNA. When viruses that match the templates enter the cell, the complementary RNA binds to them and directs a series of CRISPR-associated enzymes (Cas enzymes) to cut out the invader DNA at the binding site, making the viral threat disappear.

In 2012, French microbiologist Emmanuelle Charpentier and American biochemist Jennifer Doudna discovered that Cas enzymes, specifically Cas9, can be reprogrammed to cut nearly any part of the genome using RNA sequences made in a laboratory. Those guide RNA molecules tell Cas9 where to cut DNA in a cell. For their discovery, Charpentier and Doudna won the Nobel prize in chemistry in 2020 and the use of CRISPR has taken off in science since their breakthrough.

But scientists are still not yet close to realizing CRISPR's potential. Cas9 is great at suppressing or knocking out unwanted genes, but it's mostly not enough to cut undesirable DNA because scientists can't fully control how DNA repairs itself. Without direction, created CRDNA tends to repair itself using a method that introduces a lot of random errors, which could have very negative effects.

However, researchers have found lots of applications for CRISPR in animals like making mosquitos that can't bite or lay eggs. They've also modified plants, like creating disease-resistant corn. Scientists have also tried to bring back extinct species like the passenger pigeon back to life by changing the genomes of similar birds alive today. But when it comes to the human genome, geneticists are more hesitant. While Cas9 reliably cuts DNA where we want it to, recent experiments have shown that it can also affect genes far off target. There are also ethical concerns about using the technology to produce "designer" babies (changing a baby's eye color, for example).

CRISPR has given genetics a tool to reliably play around with our code of life, but the question of ethics and safety still remain.

Genetic testing

Genetic testing is a service that can sequence your DNA to help you find out if you have any significant changes in genes, chromosomes or proteins. The technology can help us identify our possible ancestors, diagnose, treat and predict the future course of cancer and inherited diseases, teach us about what diet serves our bodies best or even warn us about how we will react to certain medications.

In today's age, genetic testing is extremely widespread and has become an extremely commercial business. This technology may be very appealing to people because it can tell us how we can live longer and healthier lives. For example, if someone finds out that they are at-risk for diabetes, they can use the information to get help from their doctor to exercise more and eat healthier foods.

Genetic testing is made possible by the Human Genome Project that started in the 1990s. The project took more than a decade and three billion dollars to accomplish its goals, but in 2003, the team of researchers finally had the first human genome sequence. Now, tests are more widely available to the public for personal use.

Genetic tests usually use a method called genotyping, since 99.9% of human DNA is the same in every one of us. Genotyping doesn't look at all of the 3.2 billion base pairs. It only focuses on a few hundred thousand of them that makes up the 0.1% that differentiates you from others. Another method of genetic testing is whole genome sequencing (as its name suggests) or 1% whole exome sequencing (to only test the protein-coding regions of your genome). There are a wide range of other tests, including target sequencing for genes related to a certain phenotype.

However, a downside to genetic testing is that it often uses a reference genome from an individual of European origin. This means that there may be an underrepresentation of people of color in genetic studies and databases. Nevertheless, researchers still have a long way to go in perfecting these tools to encourage equality.

EXPERIMENTS

Edible marshmallow DNA model

Recommended minimum age (with parent supervision): 4 years
Note: marshmallows can be substituted with any soft candy

Materials:

- 5 Toothpicks
- 4 different colored markers
- 10 small marshmallows of one color
- 10 small marshmallows of another color

Procedures:

1. Lay out your five toothpicks and four different colored markers.
   These will represent the four nucleotide bases of DNA: Adenine,
   Thymine, Cytosine and Guanine. Select one color to represent each
   base.
   a. Because Adenine pairs with Thymine and Cytosine pairs with
      Guanine, color half of one of the toothpicks with your Adenine
      color and the other half with your Thymine color.
   b. Repeat this step for another toothpick, now using your chosen
      colors for Cytosine and Guanine.
   c. By the end of this step, you should have five toothpicks with
      alternating colors based on the pairing of DNA's four nucleotide
      bases.
2. Choose one color group of marshmallows to represent the sugar
   portion of your model's backbone. Attach one "sugar" marshmallow
   to each end of the five toothpicks.
3. The other color group of marshmallows will represent the phosphate
   portion of your model's backbone. Stick one "phosphate"
   marshmallow directly under each "sugar" marshmallow by wetting
   each end. You should now have a ladder-like structure with
   alternating colors of marshmallows running up each side of the
   model.
4. Twist the model to resemble the double helix structure of DNA!

Strawberry DNA extraction

Recommended minimum age (with parent supervision): 7 years

Materials:

- Measuring cup
- Measuring spoons
- Small bowl
- Table salt
- Water
- Dishwashing soap
- Tall drinking glass
- Small, transparent cups
- Cheesecloth
- Funnel
- 3 medium-sized strawberries
- Resealable plastic bag
- Wooden skewer
- Paper towels
- 70% Isopropyl alcohol (rubbing alcohol) chilled in the freezer for about 30 minutes

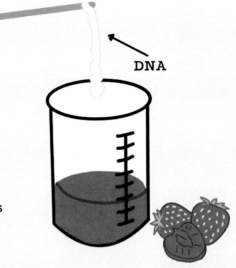

DNA

Procedures:

- Mix ⅓ cup of water, ½ teaspoon salt, and 1 tablespoon dishwashing liquid in a small bowl. This is your extraction liquid, which is what you will use to extract the DNA from the strawberries.
- Line your funnel with cheesecloth and place it into the tall, empty glass.
- Remove the green tops from the strawberries and discard them
- Place the strawberries into the resealable plastic bag. Push out the extra air and seal the bag tightly.
- Smash and squeeze the strawberries with your fingers for two minutes.
- Add 3 tablespoons of your extraction solution to the bag of strawberries and reseal the bag.
- Squeeze the strawberry mixture with your fingers for one more minute.

- Pour the strawberry mixture into the funnel.
- Let the mixture drip through the cheesecloth into the tall glass. You can squeeze the cheesecloth lightly to speed up the process (be careful, this can get a bit messy!)
- If there is a lot of foam on top of the filtered solution, let it settle before you continue the extraction.
- Transfer the filtered solution into a small, transparent cup. Fill the cup about ¼ full and remove any remaining foam.
- Add about ¼ cup of ice-cold rubbing alcohol to a small cup.
- Tilt the cup with the filtered strawberry mixture. Slowly pour the rubbing alcohol down the side of the cup.
- Pour until the alcohol layer is about the same height as the filtered strawberry mixture. Make sure the two liquids do not mix.
- Wait for five minutes and then look inside the cup. You should see a cloudy, stringy substance. This is the DNA! Extract the DNA by dipping the skewer into the cup where both solutions meet, gently swirl the skewer and then slowly pull it up to observe.

What happened?

When you added your extraction solution to the smashed strawberries, the detergent helped to lyse (or break open) the strawberry cells. This caused the cells to release their DNA into the liquid in the bag.

The salt in the extraction solution helped to create an environment where the different strands of DNA could clump together, making it easier for you to see them with your eyes. When the rubbing alcohol was added to the filtered strawberry liquid, the DNA separated from the rest of the liquid. You should have seen the cloudy DNA strands in the alcohol layer.

A single strand of DNA is too small to see with the naked eye (geneticists use microscopes to see these), but because the DNA clumped together in this experiment, you could see how much DNA three strawberries have.

Strawberries are octoploid, meaning that they have eight genomes (or eight sets of their genes), which means that it is easier to extract a large amount of DNA.

GENETICS THROUGH THE AGES

1859

On the Origin of Species is published

Charles Darwin's pioneering book describes his theory of evolution by natural selection. However, at this point, he didn't know anything about DNA's essential role in evolution because it hasn't yet been discovered!

1866

The mechanism of inheritance is explored

Austrian monk Gregor Mendel discovers that inheritance involves separate entities that we now know to be genes. Mendel's work shows that traits aren't mixed together but can instead be spread out through generations.

1869

DNA is discovered (but not quite)

Friedrich Miescher first identifies what he calls "nuclein" that we now know to be DNA. Miescher collects infected bandages from a local hospital and finds this substance in the nuclei of its human white blood cells.

1953

The double helix is defined

James Watson and Francis Crick study Rosalind Franklin's X-ray crystallography photographs and discover that DNA forms a double-helix structure. Crick is famously known for bursting into a pub in Cambridge shouting, "We have discovered the secret of life!"

1956

Hemoglobin-Beta gene mutation is identified

The mutation causing sickle cell anemia is first discovered by Vernon Ingram. The mutation, which is on chromosome 11 (see page 17), leads to the production of an abnormal version of the protein responsible for carrying oxygen in red blood cells.

1959

Down syndrome is first characterized

French physician Jérôme Lejeune identified Down syndrome as a chromosomal condition (in which the patient has 47 chromosomes).

29

1977

Speedy sequencing

Fred Sanger comes up with the idea of using the process of DNA copying to work out the order of the bases (DNA sequencing) at a high level of accuracy. Sanger's work revolutionized genetics by allowing for whole genomes to be sequenced and then compared.

1987

CRISPR first found in E. coli

Japanese scientist Yoshizumi Ishino and his team accidentally cloned an odd series of repeated sequences that contained spacers while analyzing a gene. This discovery led to the use of CRISPR and the Cas9 enzyme to create a gene-editing tool.

1989

The gene for cystic fibrosis is identified

Even though the condition was first discovered in 1938, the gene was pinpointed after advances in genetics. The Cystic Fibrosis Transmembrane Conductance Regulator (CFTR) gene was first discovered by geneticise Lap-Chee Tsui and his team.

1995

Genetic sequencing projects take off

The age of genome sequencing starts with the bacterium *Haemophilus influenzae*. The sequencing of yeast occurs in the following year. The first animal to be sequenced was *C. elegans* in 1998.

1996

Dolly the cloned sheep is born

Originally code-named "6LL3," the cloned lamb was named after actress and singer Dolly Parton at the Roslin Institute in Scotland. British developmental biologist Ian Wilmut and his colleagues used the technique of cell nuclear transfer.

2003

The Human Genome Project is completed

The first sequence of the human genome took about 13 years, involved hundreds of scientists and costs approximately $2.7 billion. The sequence provided a crucial database of information accessible to researchers worldwide for free and without restriction.

GLOSSARY

bio·mol·e·cule

noun

an organic molecule (could be a macromolecule such as a protein or nucleic acid) in living organisms.

de·oxy·ri·bo·nu·cle·ic acid

noun

often abbreviated as DNA, various nucleic acids formed of a double helix held together by hydrogen bonds between nitrogenous bases which are supported by two chains containing alternating links of deoxyribose sugar and phosphate, located solely in the nuclei of eukaryotic cells.

dip·loid

adjective

having two of each autosomal chromosome in each cell.

dom·i·nant

adjective

in genetics, of a trait or gene that masks the recessive counterpart when the two are presented together.

en·zyme

noun

any of a large number of protein s acting as catalysts (speeding-up agents) for chemical reactions with living things.

eu·kar·y·ote

noun

an organism that is composed of cell(s) that contain a membrane-bound nucleus.

ge·net·ics

noun

the scientific study of heredity, particularly of the influence of genes and DNA on the evolution, appearance and development of organisms.

hap·loid

adjective

having a single set of autosomal chromosomes. (See diploid).

he·red·i·ty

noun

the genetic transmission of traits from parent to child.

het·ero·zy·gous

adjective

pertaining to an organism with two different forms of a particular gene (allele).

ho·mol·o·gous

adjective

in genetics, having almost identical chromosome pairs, one homologous chromosome is inherited from the organism's mother and the other is inherited from the organism's father.

ho·mo·zy·gous

adjective

pertaining to an organism with a single form of a particular gene (allele).

mono·hy·brid

noun

an individual that is heterozygous (see definition) for one specific gene.

mne·mon·ic

noun

a device used to aid the memory (such as an acronym).

pal·in·drome

noun

a word (such as kayak), phrase, sentence or number (such as 1221) that reads the same backward or forward.

ped·i·gree

noun

a table or chart of ancestors often indicating descent or denoting affected individuals for a certain genetic disorder.

re·ces·sive

adjective

in genetics, of a trait or gene whose influence does not appear when presented with a masking (dominant) trait or gene.

tab·let

noun

a flat piece of stone or metal bearing an inscription.

sur·ro·gate moth·er

noun

a woman who bears a child on behalf of another individual or couple, this is typically carried out through in vitro fertilization or artificial insemination.

Made in the USA
Middletown, DE
03 October 2023

40031063R00022